THE
CHALLENGE
EFORE THE CHANGE

A Practical Approach to Overcoming the Hard Places in Life

W0008808

FRAMPTON PAUL

THE CHALLENGE BEFORE THE CHANGE
Copyright © 2018 by Frampton Paul

ISBN: 978-1-4866-1699-2

Word Alive Press
119 De Baets Street, Winnipeg, MB R2J 3R9
www.wordalivepress.ca

WORD ALIVE
—P R E S S—

Cataloguing in Publication may be obtained through Library and Archives Canada

DEDICATION

This book is for everyone who is challenged in some way, shape, or form, and on their way to being changed. My earnest wish is that you will receive an edge you never had before, or be refreshed by timely lessons you've learned before but forgotten over time. May you gain momentum and sustained perspective as you run forward—and change!

ACKNOWLEDGEMENTS

I've been privileged to have a group of wonderful people around me who make me who I am. Attempting to mention each by name would quickly, without question, become a book unto itself. However, my sincere thanks to all who've shared and assisted in the birthing phase of this project. You know who you are.

To my mentors, administrative team, leaders, and partners, thank you for believing in the person I've been blessed to be and serve.

CONTENTS

FOREWORD

It would take more than a minute to reminisce about the span of events that has limned your life, wouldn't it? In the single moment it took you to read that opening line, did an emotion grip you? Did you feel grateful, happy, sad, frustrated, angry, confused, or possibly challenged by the blurred events of your life?

We live and we learn; we learn and we live. It's the learning curve that challenges us most. In fact, when learning curves turn to challenging moments, we fret. And when change seems a long way off, we question: why is this happening to me?

Author Polly B. Berends has said, "Everything that happens to you is your teacher. The secret is to learn to sit at the feet of your own life and be taught by it."[1]

The last thing we want when we are in the battle of challenge and change is the boring complication of a classroom. We want personal interaction from someone who will, in the

---

1 Polly Berrien Berends, "Everything that happens…" *Goodreads.* Date of access: April 3, 2018 (https://www.goodreads.com/quotes/61047-everything-that-happens-to-you-is-your-teacher-the-secret).

most practical way, help us make sense of the clueless go-ings-on in our private world.

Frampton Paul does this very well. Like a compassionate friend, he sits across from us and holds a candid conversation on how we should face our life challenges. He speaks straight, directly, and affirms us.

He brings us alongside Jesus and invites us to take a journey with Him to ancient Jericho, where He encountered a unique fella by the name of Zacchaeus. We get to see that his life was very similar to some of ours today.

As Frampton unpacks for us the events of the Jesus-Zac-chaeus encounter, he shares with intrigue and hope how we, too, can get beyond any challenge we may be facing in our lives, past, present, or even those to come.

I read this book twice in one setting. When I was done, I looked up to heaven and said, "Lord, I welcome challenge and I welcome change!" I'm not a betting man, but if I were I'd bet that you, too, might just look up and say what I said.

Thank you, Frampton, for a very insightful chat from the Book of books and the Lord of Change, Jesus.

The Zacchaeuses of today, like me and many others, are ready to encounter Him!

—Walter Boston, Jr.

Walter Boston, Jr. Ministries, Inc.

Charlotte, North Carolina

INTRODUCTION

God is looking for some good men and women, children, and youth. He needs an ark builder, a Noah, or an Abraham, someone who has received an instruction from the Lord and is building something—a life, a family, personal character, a house, a business, or a ministry. To Abraham, the Lord said, paraphrased, "Go separate yourself. Go into the direction that I will show you."

When the Lord spoke with Abraham in Genesis 12, God introduced him to a new set of challenges. Everything Abraham knew was about to be shifted in order for him to receive the promise spoken by the Lord. That in itself can be a huge challenge. Things don't always make sense at the beginning. As a matter of fact, challenging situations often don't seem to add up at first sight. By taking several steps in the right direction, however, Abraham and his entire household later understood the good of their challenges.

I also want to encourage the Isaacs among us, those who are in the process of moving in the direction of the Holy Spirit. The Bible helps us understand in the book of Genesis that Isaac's herdsmen and the Philistines struggled for access to wells. At the end of the struggle, Isaac came to settle in Rehoboth—meaning, a large place, room without restraint. Can you imagine it? One moment they were arguing and quarreling about wells. In the days following, they came to a place with an abundance of land for more wells!

I want to also encourage a Daniel. After the king signed a decree outlawing the worship of any other god but him, after everything had been said and settled, Daniel continued to pray and open his windows three times a day, as was his usual custom. He did this despite what the king had said. Perhaps you, too, have decided in your spirit that you are going to go ahead and do the will of God.

I want to stand with a Shadrach, Meshach, and Abednego. I want to stand with you, not in your fiery furnace, as it were, but to let you know that there are people who are going through the same things and are not bowing.

I want to stand with a Jacob, and be an encourager to him. He was the one who wrestled with God and didn't give up until his name was changed. He didn't give up until he heard that his name would no longer be called Jacob but would be called Israel, for as a prince he had obtained favor with God and with man.

How challenging it must have been for Jacob, even before that night of human struggle against divine force. Throughout

Genesis, we see Jacob's life riddled with the complexities of family, friends, and foes. Yet he inched closer with each passing day until his life was transformed.

I'm looking for a Zerrubabel and Nehemiah—someone who is deliberate in restoring direction, focus, and spiritual order.

I want to encourage you, like Zerrubabel was encouraged as he led an expedition to go back into Jerusalem for the re-building of the temple, and like Nehemiah, who was found praying and seeking God about the nation of Israel before rebuilding the walls. But what are you going to do as far as rebuilding the sacred walls of your life, and the sacred walls of the lives of others and those of your family, ministry, church, and community?

I want to speak to you, God's chosen men and women today. Like David, a shepherd boy with a heart of gold and the holy boldness to take on the giant, you may be someone who seems naive, yet the anointing, the oil of God, is poured and flowing upon you.

I want to speak to an apostle Paul. I want to come along-side someone who is walking with the Lord but who is yet to say, "I have fought the good fight, I have kept the faith." I want to walk with you! Walking through life might be simple for some, but for others it can be trying, even very challenging.

We are all confronted with challenges: how to live, where and for whom to work, who to love, where to worship… The lists may be endless, and very often the questions are overwhelming. However, let's pull back some timely lessons and great truths taken from Jesus's unusual encounter with Zacchaeus.

Today, let's discover the challenge before the change.

The Exhortation

Here's the first thing I want you to know: your challenge is temporary.

Many people are praying and believing God right now that certain things in their lives will change. Many are hoping that a prophet will come along and prophesy change into their lives. But the truth of the matter is that while a prophet may prophesy change and let you know about the favor and blessing of God upon your life, there's always a challenge that precedes change.

You are reading this right now and everything seems to be falling apart. Wherever you are in this given year, you have seen more challenges than change almost every year. You have prayed and sought the Lord. You have stayed humble and have even sought God through fasting. You are asking God, "When am I going to experience my change? When are things going to level out for me? When am I going to inherit my Promised Land?"

The Lord has instructed me to tell you that the change is on its way, but we must all face the challenge before the change.

Let us take a look at a very familiar portion of Scripture: *"And Jesus entered and passed through Jericho. And, behold, there was a man named Zacchaeus, which was the chief among the publicans, and he was rich"* (Luke 19:1–2, KJV)

This may not sound like you, or it may not sound like anybody you know, but stay with me, as there is a lesson for us to learn in this story.

> *And he sought to see Jesus who he was; and could not for the press, because he was little of stature. And he ran before, and climbed up into a sycomore tree to see him: for he was to pass that way. And when Jesus came to the place, he looked up, and saw him, and said unto him, Zacchaeus, make haste, and come down; for to day I must abide at thy house. And he made haste, and came down, and received him joyfully.*
>
> —Luke 19:3–6, KJV

Jesus entered Jericho for several reasons, but one of the most pressing reasons was Zacchaeus himself.

Jesus has entered your country, your neighborhood, your village, and your house today. Why? The reason is for you! Specifically for you. I want to get this into your spirit: despite where you are, Jesus is paying you a visit right now. This isn't just about sharing a word with you; Jesus is paying you a visit now.

When Jesus entered Jericho, so many people followed Him. Crowds always followed Jesus. Wherever He went, whenever He entered a city, crowds pressed Him from all angles.

But there was one person in that crowd in Jericho who didn't want a mere visit from Jesus. Zacchaeus wanted to see Jesus, and he wanted to experience change! He was willing to do whatever it took, give whatever it would cost him, to change. Whatever the sacrifice, he was willing to make the sacrifice. He was willing to make the sacrifice to see Jesus Christ of Nazareth. Jesus had come into his town, into his neighborhood, and he was ready.

Here's the question: when Jesus pays you a visit, will you be ready? Will you be ready when Jesus shows up? Will you be ready when Jesus shows up in the form of a preacher, in the form of a common person, in the form of a circumstance or situation? Will you be willing to see Jesus?

Challenges can be unpredictable. Depending on the nature of the challenge, it can be brutal, and sadly devastating.

Once news of Jesus's arrival into Jericho came to Zacchaeus, something began to happen inside him. While there were challenges that Zacchaeus had to contend with, though, he had a desire to see Jesus.

Here's the point: challenges have the power to alter our desires. We don't all handle the unknown, the harsh, or the unfavorable in the same way. However, when we confront the unknown we are presented with a tremendous opportunity to muster up the faith and courage to ignite a powerful sense of desire for the next phase in our lives.

Jesus's arrival to Jericho introduced a brand-new phase for the people there, and particularly in Zacchaeus. We are told in Luke 19:3, *"And he sought to see Jesus who he was"* (KJV). The presence of Jesus birthed a desire in the heart and mind of this total stranger. The fact that Zacchaeus sought to see Jesus indicates the level of impact Jesus had already made on someone who hadn't even seen him.

But we are informed of Zacchaeus's real challenge: *"[he] could not for the press, because he was little of stature"* (Luke 19:3, KJV).

So what will you learn from this point forward with regards to where you are, what you desire, and what you are willing to do?

CHALLENGES DEMAND THAT WE MAKE GREAT SACRIFICES

The Bible says that Zacchaeus heard Jesus was in the neighborhood, and the text shows the degree of his desperation. Zacchaeus was so desperate to see Jesus that nothing could hinder him from seeing Jesus.

Let this sink into your spirit. There is always a challenge, or challenges, before the change. There will always be broken things before the last thing gets mended. Things often get worse before they get better.

I hope you fully comprehend this. I want to encourage you today, my dear friend, to do whatever it takes to overcome every challenge you are facing today. Or better yet, find the courage to cope with the challenge you are facing.

I'm sure you can identify with this situation. Sometimes you receive a prophetic word, but before it can come to pass, everything that can go wrong will go wrong. We sometimes say that the devil is a liar and that satan isn't going to do this or that, but the fact of the matter is that satan doesn't have to do anything. But challenges will still come.

EVERY CHALLENGE IS UNIQUE TO YOU

Although there had been challenges in Jericho before Jesus passed through, there were some that were unique to Zacchaeus. What were the main challenges he had when Jesus came to Jericho?

First of all, Zacchaeus was a man of little stature. That placed him in a particular group: the category of short people. He did not stand head and shoulders above the crowd. In other words, if he had to gain a good view, he had to get to a place where he would be *elevated*.

I want you to guard this word in your spirit. When Jesus comes to your neighborhood, He comes with the intention and purpose of *elevating* you. It may not seem to you like elevation is coming, but I want to let you know, my friend, that elevation is right around the corner. You might be in the valley today—you might be the shortest person who ever existed, your circumstances might be short, you might be short financially, or short in your spirit, short in your patience, short in your faith, short in everything—but I come with this message: elevation is coming!

This was one of the main setbacks Zacchaeus faced. His height created a dilemma and challenge.

There are many people who feel that their physical height or physiology creates a challenge. Many people say that they cannot accomplish certain things because they feel that they are too short or too skinny. They begin to think about their appearance, even their hair color or texture, as a challenge.

I want to encourage you that none of these things, as challenging as they may seem, sound, or feel, can prevent Jesus from elevating you. While challenges may slow you down, if you respond to them correctly they won't stop you from making purposeful change. There is a sure elevation on the way, and it is coming because Jesus has come close to you.

When Jesus came to Jericho, He came with Zacchaeus in mind. Zacchaeus was on His agenda. Some people may beg to differ. Let us suppose that Zacchaeus was not on Jesus's agenda, but instead Jesus was on Zacchaeus's agenda!

Let me take you one step further, to stretch your sanctified imagination. Imagine that you are trying to see someone, but no matter how hard you try you are hindered, whether by red tape or bureaucracy. Everything is standing between you and this person, especially if it's someone of influence and clout.

Nevertheless, I'm talking to someone today who has stubborn faith. You're going to face your challenges head-on. Whatever challenge you are facing now, I speak into your spirit as you read these words: I tell you that this challenge has only come because your change is around the corner. It doesn't matter how structured things may be, for God is able to penetrate any structure. God is able to go through any hierarchy, able to break through any bureaucracy.

Zacchaeus's determination brought him close enough that his heart began to pump. His heart pumped a little faster and his mind raced. Can you imagine the sweat on Zacchaeus's brow? Can you feel the anxiety and imagine the thoughts that must have been going around in his head? Can you picture what he might have been saying to himself? "I have a challenge ahead of me. I am too short and the crowd is too big. Plus, Jesus is surrounded by His disciples. Am I going to see Jesus?"

However, Zacchaeus may then have said something different to himself, "This is just a challenge. I am going to move into that challenge because beyond every challenge is a change."

Interestingly, every challenge comes with a specific assignment. But are we ready to yield to the assignments which every challenge brings? The truth is, the more difficult the challenge, the more apparent and resourceful the change.

YOUR CHALLENGE IS SHAPING YOU FOR THE BETTER

Once we recognize that challenges are change agents, we can begin to envision that our change is right around the corner. Had Zacchaeus known how close he was to really seeing Jesus? The provision of God is much closer than your challenges. Every struggle you're facing now is shaping you for the success God has in store for you. Every blessing the Father has for you is preceded by many challenges. The way you handle each one determines what happens next.

As we continue, we see that Zacchaeus had another challenge: the size of the crowd. If being short wasn't bad enough, the multitude which followed Jesus from other cities descended upon this minute-statured man in an unbelievable way. In order to see Jesus, he had to be close enough to have a clear view. This, of course, was impossible.

Yes, sometimes challenges appear to be impossible. Things seem to be etched in stone, or set on a particular course of no return.

Perhaps that's exactly where you find yourself today, in a crowded environment with lots of activity but very little productivity. This is a real battle for you. I understand. Even the simplest things can be obstructed when you are in a crowded place. Access is often limited, and resources are often restricted. Usually the ones who seem to have the advantage, who get the benefits, are the ones who've understood how to overcome the challenges of being in a crowd.

So how did Zacchaeus deal with the crowd challenge? Despite the crowd, despite his height, the Bible says that Zacchaeus did something that many of us might not have thought to do. Zacchaeus said to himself, "I'm going to run ahead and climb a tree."

I am speaking directly to someone today: the only way that change is going to come for you is if you are willing to do what others would not be willing to do. You have to be willing to move into a direction that others may not desire to move into. You must be willing to move at a pace others aren't willing to move at. You may have to make these tough choices if you're going to break free and break through the challenges of your life.

I propose to you, on the authority of God's Word, that unless we are willing to walk alone, we aren't ready to lead or achieve anything of significance. We aren't ready to be distinguished, let alone conquer any challenge we encounter.

Unless you are willing to do something differently, you are not ready for change. Change operates in a particular mold and change knows a particular mindset. Change fuels us from a different perspective, allowing us to think and act differently. Change breaks the norm of whatever you are accustomed to. Change is out to break that norm. God is the only constant in the universe, and He is unchangeable (Malachi 3:6).

The ability to overcome his challenges required Zacchaeus to desire differently. He wasn't the only height-challenged individual in Jericho, but his desire to see Jesus gave him an immediate advantage. We experience an immediate advantage once we mentally shift our desires. That's when things begin to come together.

Your desire, or lack thereof, has power. If your desire is channeled in the proper direction, you will become a force which disarms the very things that are limiting others. As a matter of fact, limits are placed in our minds before they exist anywhere else. Hence, we need to disarm our thoughts if we're going to embrace lasting change.

To overcome his challenge, Zacchaeus had to make a decision. As important as it is to have a desire, every desire dies prematurely when no decision gets made. When we make a decision, it builds on the foundation of our desire and helps us to create a plan. Zacchaeus decided that it was time to run! Once Zacchaeus ran ahead, the crowd was no longer a challenge to him.

You can only maneuver and advance beyond certain situations in life when you're willing to move into new areas. Some of these new areas may not be acceptable or comfortable, but once you have the direction of the Lord, your greatest challenge can suddenly be your greatest breakthrough. We can never experience lasting change unless we courageously push through the very things that are pushing back at us.

Here we have a man who was handicapped by a situation beyond his control. Yet he didn't roll over and pity himself. His mustered his courage, fired up a plan, and executed that plan while others were still thinking about seeing Jesus.

The fact remains that others may have seen him running. What was there reaction to his exercise of faith? Was he discouraged or ridiculed? We don't have that sort of information, but I'm moved to believe that he may have had his critics, or even a few enemies. Based on the fact that he was a tax collector, he wasn't liked by some people. Nonetheless, he began his run. Running, for Zacchaeus, meant handling his challenge in a changed way.

What keep Zacchaeus steady on his path was his desire, his decision, and the direction in which he chose to run. I find it rather encouraging that the Scripture tells us, in Luke 19:4, *"So he ran on ahead..."* (ESV)

His decision was important, as was his decision *when* to run. There seemed to be no delay on His part. He thought it, he envisioned it—he saw himself running, he saw himself ahead of the crowd—and he engaged the moment as his last best chance of seeing Jesus.

But the direction in which he decided to run made a world of difference. He ran *ahead*—not alongside the crowd, not behind them, and not with them—understanding that others may try to keep up with the crowd.

The direction you take is important when you're confronted by the hard stuff of life. Truthfully, many challenges never disappear. A forty-year-old man doesn't miraculously move from four and a half feet to six feet tall. At least, I've not seen it happen. Some things don't change overnight. With the proper timing, the right momentum, and a dash of diligence, change will inevitably take place.

But here's what you and I can see: our decisions and our direction.

I've thought about this long and hard. What would have happened had Zacchaeus brought along a couple of running buddies? What would have been the result should he have decided to run alongside the crowd? How about running in the opposite direction?[2]

---

2   Well, this one is so obvious that even a child knows the answer: Zacchaeus would have run into even greater challenges and eventually missed his change. Yes, his change!

We must sometimes make even the toughest decision alone. Of course, I'm not suggesting that we should rely solely on our noble ideas to navigate the vicissitudes of life. However, we have before us an example of confident trust. Zacchaeus had to learn to trust his own heart—ultimately, the voice of the Spirit.

At this point, this great man didn't need to make a height adjustment; he had to adjust his internal, spiritual, mental stature. Life takes on an entirely new meaning when we grow mentally and emotionally. And oftentimes challenges force us into that dimension of change. And Zacchaeus was about to get real tall from the inside-out.

Can you imagine what really changes when our perspective changes? New things, better things, great things begin to emerge.

So he ran ahead, but what he did next is even more important. He climbed a tree! When was the last time you climbed a tree? Maybe when you were a kid, if you lived in an area with trees around you.

It's a good thing to climb trees, especially when they can lift you above your challenges. I'm not referring to actual trees, but figurative ones. We have to come into a mindset that takes us higher—higher than the noise, higher than the norm. In fact, take a climb that lifts you so high that your challenges completely fade beneath you.

Unless you've received the change you long for, unless you have seen the manifestation of that which was already written in heaven by God, you have a right to pursue, push, and carry on your prescribed course of action without fail.

Ultimately, it's up to you: do you desire to see Jesus? After Zacchaeus had separated himself from the crowd, he didn't stop there. He continued to use his creative ability to put himself in a place of advantage, by climbing the tree. Note well that the tree was also a place of great access. At that altitude, his view ushered him into a space others didn't possess.

While people often share similar challenges, it's only those who demonstrate a different attitude toward their situations and take charge over them who are privileged to move into an entirely new domain.

Consequently, there's always a better place in every challenging situation. There's a place of advantage. Every challenge has an advantage connected to it which can be discovered if we pay attention.

It was his decision which brought him to the place where he could *see* Jesus. Are you at the beginning of a decision with regards to a challenge? Are you halfway? Or have you gone so far that you're about to taste the victory of your God-directed efforts?

Running ahead and climbing a tree represented just a fraction of a step in the right direction for Zacchaeus. So much truth flows from this encounter with Zacchaeus, a man of simple action yet great faith. It's amazing how simple actions can transform our world.

Now that he was perched on that tree, why was he there? Yes, his intention was clear: he wanted to see Jesus! But why a sycamore tree? Were there any other trees? Why this particular sycamore? Was it because of its form or position?

Here's what John Gill, a Bible commentator, has remarked about sycamore trees that

> their branches were large; and this is the reason why Zacchaeus went up into one of these trees, because it was large and able to bear him, and tall, from whence he could have a full view of Christ.[3]

We may not have the evidence to piece it all together, but one thing is sure: Zacchaeus's decision to move in the right direction by no means disappointed him.

Isn't it wonderful that you can make a decision which puts you exactly where you are supposed to be at the right time?

---

3   John Gill, *Gill's Exposition of the Entire Bible* from *BibleHub*, "Commentaries, Luke 19.4." Date of access: April 12, 2018 (http://biblehub.com/commentaries/luke/19-4.htm).

Let's think about this for a moment. How did he feel, knowing that he had accomplished this task of faith and his view of Jesus had become so much clearer? After all, his challenge had been shifted, because he had been changed through the process. Zacchaeus was no longer obstructed by the crowd. He had left them far behind. He was no longer limited by his height. He was far above everyone else, sitting in the tree.

Who would have thought that a few challenges would have worked in Zacchaeus's favor? This is another reason why we can't allow our challenges to keep us on the sidelines.

As important as it was for Jesus to have visited Jericho, the real impact was quickly taking place because a man was being changed in the process.

In Zacchaeus's case, he didn't leave anything to chance. It was no accident, but rather it was woven gracefully by the certain leading of the promise of the Spirit. Zacchaeus had found the right tree, the right branch, the right spot... and now the right moment.

The time had come for him to see from a different angle!

Challenges Allow You See Life from a Different Vantage Point

That word *see*, although it refers to natural sight, conveys another meaning: to gain a better understanding of someone or something. I want us to go deeper as we gain a better understanding of what took place when Zacchaeus encountered Jesus.

The Bible says that Zacchaeus wanted to see Jesus, but this was about something more than just glimpsing Him with his eyes. Zacchaeus wanted an experience with Jesus. Better yet, he wanted an encounter. Deep within his heart, he had an urgent longing to connect with the Lord of Lords and King of Kings, to connect in a way that he had never connected with anyone else.

Out of this connection, his life would change. Thus far, a few things had changed. His perspective had changed. His location had changed. His desires and decision had changed. Now his life was about to be change!

A huge part of that sense of reformation would be the birthing of new covenant connections.

CHALLENGES OFTEN BIRTH NEW COVENANT CONNECTIONS

You may think that Zacchaeus only wanted a casual glance at Jesus. I beg to differ. He wanted a detailed and undistracted view of the Master. He wanted to see—or rather, experience for himself—the Man who had done so many mighty works throughout the region's cities, towns, and villages. He wanted an encounter with the One who saw further ahead than the crowd. He wanted the Jesus who also wanted to see him!

We need to see Jesus with more than our natural eyes, to experience Him beyond our senses. We need to experience Him in the spirit. This is what Zacchaeus desired, and his decision to run ahead placed him in the right position. At that instant, in the tree, he had faced every challenge head-on and was released into the wind of change.

Challenges can be unbearable. They can be emotionally draining—and worst of all, even discouraging. However, when we gain fresh perspective, challenges become like fuel. They stir up a new wave of thinking. They give us a new sense of urgency. They don't let us succumb to the ills of the present, not when a glorious and brighter future lies ahead.

Although life challenged Zacchaeus, at that moment he was willing to challenge everything and everyone. That's often the missing element for us. How are we going to use what's up against us to motivate and activate in us the very things we never thought we had?

Let me put it to you this way: the change you desire may require some drastic measures on your part. It may mean that you have to run ahead of your friends and family. It may mean that you have to distance yourself from the crowd, even some so-called friends, family members, and co-workers—anyone who will hinder you from moving toward a more fulfilling and productive end.

There is a "tree" for all of us, especially for those who are in the middle of unattractive situations. You've got to decide to fuel your next leg of your life journey by using the very things that are a challenge to you.

Certain crowds will work for you as long as you work with them, but the moment you decide to blaze a new trail, to move in a new direction and dream your own dreams, to put on your own shoes and dress in your own coat, they will come up against you. You will be faced with a challenge.

Zacchaeus was willing and determined to pay the price, unlike most in the crowd, so he ran ahead. The Bible describes Zacchaeus jetting ahead of the crowd because Jesus was already in the neighbourhood.

"I need to see Jesus," Zacchaeus said.

You know, there's a difference between *wanting* to see Jesus and *needing* to see Jesus. When you want something, you can do without it. You don't need it to survive.

Today I'm speaking to you whose challenge is so great that you don't want an experience with Jesus. You *need* an experience with Jesus. The presence of Jesus is going to shift everything for you, and it's going to mean more than survival; it's going to elevate you. Something is going to happen for you.

THERE'S A WAY OUT OF EVERY CHALLENGE

Isn't it amazing that despite how challenging our circumstances may be, there is always a way out? Think about how long Noah had to build the ark, how long he had to preach. Who knows how tired Noah became day by day of obediently going after his God-given command to prepare for the heavy rain? But Noah kept building, he kept on preaching, and he kept moving forward.

I want to encourage you today. No matter how steep the challenge may be, keep on moving forward, as there is always a way out of the challenge. A change is bound to come.

Abraham experienced challenges as he moved in the direction God told him to move. Abraham made errors for a while; he went to Egypt, and he also had a child with his maid, under his wife's instruction, as they both feared that they would never have a child. But then Abraham got back on course and took the bull by the horns. He conquered every other challenge and followed God's instructions wholeheartedly until he died.

The challenge will come before the change, but we must find trees to climb and follow the Lord completely. Trees are like access points. In every challenge, God will give you a point of access. You may want to call it an exit. Call it whatever you want, but there is always something, a ladder placed here on earth like in Jacob's dream. These trees or ladders will give you divine access into heaven, access to everything you need to face your coming life change.

Zacchaeus wanted to see Jesus, so he ascended the tree. Today, God wants you to mount up upon every challenge you face.

As John 10:10 teaches us, *"The thief cometh not, but for to steal, and to kill, and to destroy"* (KJV). The challenge is not the thief, but it's a test. The majority of challenges you face—be they family, friends, foes, colleagues, employers or employees, spouses or children—do not come to kill you; they come to allow you to ascend, to rise up, to build you!

When Jesus was crucified and then buried, the Bible says that on the third day He rose. And a few days later, the Bible says that He ascended. The challenge of dying on the cross, of being placed in a borrowed tomb, of having to be resurrected, didn't stop Him from having the power to ascend. Amen!

CHALLENGES WILL CAUSE YOU TO ASCEND

Every challenge you and I face is presented to give us leverage. Did you know that every valley is followed by a climb, and that climb eventually takes you to a mesa, plateau, or mountaintop. Once you experience a valley, the next thing you're going to experience is an incline. Then it's time for us to get ready to ascend. We cannot be elevated unless we go through and embrace our challenges. We're not qualified to be the recipients of significant change unless we've handled the challenges in our lives with fortitude.

I want to take you on a journey today. These words are here to encourage you. We cannot experience our ascension unless we mount up on our challenges. I want you to comprehend this.

How do most of us respond to our challenges? Many people cry. Others ask, why? I want to help you today. The next time you're facing something, don't ask why. There are times when you'll have to cry, but don't panic. Find something in your spirit that says, "Hey, this one is going to push me higher." Say it with me right now: "This challenge is going to push me higher."

The challenges Zacchaeus faced were created by the infinite wisdom of God, and they were challenges that were designed to take him higher. Remember that he was a man of little stature and a man who had to contend with a crowd that was preventing him from accessing Jesus. In that situation, God deposited in his spirit a strategy; God gave him a way out. Zacchaeus then moved ahead of the crowd and said, "I am going to ascend. I'm going to climb that tree."

Think about this, friends: if we're quiet enough, if we're still enough, if we're passionate enough, if we're enthusiastic enough, if we dream long enough, and if we're determined or persistent enough, our challenges will create for us doorways of breakthrough, blessing, favor, and supernatural possibilities. You couldn't access some things because you didn't look around, or you thought they weren't available. But if you could only allow your challenge to talk to you, you would find the answer.

We must learn to let our challenges speak. If someone raises their heel against you, it's time to let your challenge begin to talk. Your challenge is going to create an access point. It's going to show you a point of elevation. It will show you the door!

For example, if you're in a boat or ship and it's taking in water, perhaps you're in the lower part of the ship and you can see the water coming in. This creates a challenge for you, for you know that the ship is going to sink if it continues to take in water. If you remain where you are, you may drown.

But as the Spirit of the Lord empowers you, you see the water coming and you say, "This is a challenge, something that has come to threaten my life. But I declare that I have the power to use this as a means of ascent."

So what do you do? You see the water coming in and you have several options. You could find a container and begin to bale the water out. Or you could ascend from the lower part of the vessel to the higher part. If you do this, the challenge has moved you up from a place of chaos, a place of struggle, a place of confusion, and worst of all a place where you didn't know what to do. Basically, after finding yourself engulfed in water, you have managed to reach the top.

God wants us to get to a state where we stand atop our challenges. That's why the Bible says we will be made the head and not the tail:

> *And the Lord shall make thee the head, and not the tail; and thou shalt be above only, and thou shalt not be beneath; if that thou hearken unto the commandments of the Lord thy God, which I command thee this day, to observe and to do them. . .*
>
> —Deuteronomy 28:13, KJV

There is no reason that your challenge should be on top of you! Whenever a challenge presents itself, know that this is your time to look around and say to yourself, "There must be a ladder, there must be a rope, there must be a tree. There must be something that is going to help me to ascend."

Zacchaeus found himself a tree. What are you going to find?

This tree was rather unique when it came to the position of its branches. They were easily accessible. Can you see how the Lord will make a way to bring you out, bring you through, and most importantly lift you up? He will elevate you! When God is ready to change your situation, no amount of challenge can block His hand. In the same way that He made a way through the Red Sea for the Hebrews, He will make a way for you.

The Bible says, *"Behold, I will do a new thing; now it shall spring forth; shall ye not know it? I will even make a way in the wilderness, and rivers in the desert"* (Isaiah 43:19).

But your heart must be ready to follow His lead. Zacchaeus's way was made the moment that the Lord allowed him to move beyond the masses. Finding the tree was his interlude to a phase of life he hadn't yet experienced.

We live our lives in stages. There will be moments of inadequacies, moments of opposition or difficulties, and moments of revelation. There will be times when all you see is darkness, the crowd, and your inability to be and do. But things can change; things must change.

In our moment of revelation, we may still have to push, exert new strength, reach new goals, and take on tasks we hadn't planned on. That's all part of the change. No matter how small the change may be, it's an indication that God has something better in mind for you.

When God makes a way, there is no time for reasoning, and there is no time for excuses. It is time to act. There is no time for indecision. We must find what God has made available to us, and by faith begin to ascend. See yourself in the spirit putting one foot to the left and one foot to the right and then continuing up, grabbing the branches in the name of Jesus and pulling yourself up. It's time that you begin to pull yourself out of your challenging situation and begin to run. But you're not running *from* your challenges; instead you'll be running *into* your change.

As Zacchaeus began to run from the crowd, think about what he may have been saying to the challenge: "You may precede my change, you may come before the change I anticipate, you may come before the breakthrough I need, and you may come before what God is going to do in my life, but it doesn't matter. Guess what? You are not going to stop me!"

Be assured in your heart that whatever your challenge has presented to you, it is not enough to stop you—and you should not allow it to stop you.

We don't have to look very far to understand what it would have been like if Zacchaeus had remained in the crowd. How would his life have been impacted had he settled for the challenges he faced? While we may never know the actual outcome, we may very well argue that his desire to see Jesus would have quickly been overrun by a more advantaged crowd.

I'm speaking to a church-planter right now. I'm speaking to a missionary. I'm speaking to a worship leader. I'm speaking to a musician. I'm speaking to someone who has no connection with the church, and I'm speaking to somebody who is trying to find their way through life—perhaps a student, a janitor, or even a security guard. I'm talking to you. Wherever you have found yourself in life, even beyond the worst of situations, whether it be a family situation, health problem, or financial crisis, I want to say to you in the name of Jesus, "It is time to rise up above your challenge. Find the tree!"

The Holy Scriptures contain many references regarding trees. For example, we read in Psalm 1:3,

And he shall be like a tree planted by the rivers of water, that bringeth forth his fruit in his season; his leaf also shall not wither; and whatsoever he doeth shall prosper. (KJV)

Exodus 15 contains another example. When the waters were bitter, the Lord showed Moses a tree in the wilderness— of all places, a tree is in the wilderness! Moses took a branch from that tree, broke it, and dropped it into the water. Do you know what happened? The water was transformed (changed).

> *And when they came to Marah, they could not drink of the*
> *waters of Marah, for they were bitter: therefore the name of it*
> *was called Marah. And the people murmured against Moses,*
> *saying, What shall we drink? And he cried unto the Lord; and*
> *the Lord shewed him a tree, which when he had cast into the*
> *waters, the waters were made sweet: there he made for them a*
> *statute and an ordinance, and there he proved them. . .*
>
> —Exodus 15:23–25, KJV

I came with this word to tell you that the change you are anticipating is right around the corner. As a matter of fact, your challenge has created its own outlet of change. That's right: your challenge has created its own outlet of change!

When the children of Israel were in the wilderness, they were thirsty. Then they began to murmur amongst themselves and against Moses. That was, of course, a challenge by itself. Moses was challenged by the people's murmuring. The people began to complain, whine, and worry. In fact, they started to drive Moses crazy. Do you know what Moses did? He turned to God and told Him exactly what he was facing.

It was a challenge, my friends, but this challenge birthed a change in the wilderness. I want you to remember that your challenge is going to create its very own outlet of change.

Zacchaeus found a tree and said to himself that nothing would prevent him from seeing Jesus. Nothing would prevent him from experiencing the depth he needed to experience, and nothing would prevent him from receiving the touch of glory he desired to receive.

Let's join Zacchaeus and say, "By God's grace, absolutely nothing will prevent me from serving God faithfully. It doesn't matter who wants to give up, or who wants to turn back or go away. It doesn't matter who wants to gossip, criticize, or waste their time whining, murmuring, or losing courage and focus. It doesn't matter if you don't want to see Jesus. But I am going to see Jesus! I am going to have an experience of a lifetime with Him."

I invite you to come along for the journey. We are following in the footsteps of Zacchaeus.

Challenges Create Experiences You've Never Had Before

One of the things challenges do for us is they create pockets of experiences we've never had. There are certain things I could not have experienced unless I had been through certain challenges.

For example, you cannot know the healing power of God unless you've been sick. You won't have a testimony of the healing power of God unless you've been able to brush shoulders with a sickness beyond a common cold. I'm talking about a sickness that posed a threat to your life. I'm talking about someone who has come back from a life-threatening situation and can say: "Guess what? I've been challenged to the point where the doctors gave up on me, but God made me experience something I would have never experienced had it not been for that kind of challenge."

If you feel that you're in a place where you are challenged in every area of your life, where everything that can go wrong has gone wrong, I have news for you. As a servant of God, stand flatfooted and run ahead, because there is a tree that will allow you to ascend. God is going to allow you to rise above your challenge.

Yes, I'm speaking directly to you. God knew that you would read this book this day and that your change would be revealed to you!

This reminds me of the scenario where the disciples were in the storm and Jesus appeared to them walking on water. Everybody thought they were going under, but Jesus showed them that in the midst of a storm is the time to learn to walk on water. It's not the time to learn to swim or think of drowning, because when you're in a storm you need to lift up your feet and step upon the waves.

Jesus is beside you in the storm of your life, so step onto the water and begin to walk on through the storm in the name of Jesus Christ. Move out in faith!

I am talking to you, dear friend. Wherever you have found yourself, with all that has gone wrong and is still going wrong, I want you to know that your change is coming. There is a tree at the right location, placed strategically just for you.

There is someone God has assigned to lift you up. I want you to believe that God has assigned me to lift you up today. Your spirit might be cast down, but I am here to lift your spirit up. I am here to pull you up from that challenge. The Word of God is today your tree; seize it and ascend to the heights God wants you to reach.

From the moment Zacchaeus climbed the tree, from the moment when he embraced the reality that the tree was going to help him, when he realized that the help he needed would come from that particular tree, he said to himself, "My change has come. I'm in a better place and my challenges are no more!"

Just know that your challenges begin to fail the moment you begin to see the tree. That's the moment when you begin to see things differently. The very moment when your spirit takes hold of the reality that there is a tree up ahead, and that it is a tree you can climb, a change is being wrought. It may be that the tree is a little further than you can see right now, and all you can see is the outline in the distance, but I want to encourage you to keep running towards it. As soon as you get to the tree, grasp the trunk and climb. Let this be a tree of hope, one of purpose and destiny.

CHANGE COMES WHEN THE CHALLENGE IS CONQUERED

The Bible tells us that Zacchaeus was well-perched between the branches of the sycamore tree when Jesus came.

The real change you are seeking is going to find you. I know that many people go on a pursuit to find things, and there's nothing wrong with that, for the Bible says, "Seek and you shall find." Here are the exact words of the Master: *"And I say unto you, Ask, and it shall be given you; seek, and ye shall find; knock, and it shall be opened unto you"* (Luke 11:9, KJV).

This is a scriptural principle. Zacchaeus had to run ahead to find the tree; that was the sacrificial part.

However, there is a part we cannot do. We must always learn to do our part and play our part, but we must acknowledge that there are some things we aren't able to do. Zacchaeus could not bring Jesus to himself! The Bible mentions that Jesus had to pass that way. There is always something that has to pass in the direction where you are. There is always someone that has to move in the direction of the tree you're now holding on to.

My dear friends, while Zacchaeus was in that tree the Holy Word says that Jesus came. Did you know that the change you're anticipating, desiring, and hoping for is going to meet up with you? I feel it so powerfully in my spirit. The change is about to catch up with you. That thing you have been praying for, that breakthrough, that power, that anointing, that wisdom, that grace, that understanding… it's about to catch up with you. That deeper walk with Jesus is coming. God heard when you said that you needed more of Him and less of yourself. It will all catch up with you because you have done your part by running ahead and ascending the tree. You've made the preparation. You've done your part.

Psalm 24:3 asks, *"Who shall ascend into the hill of the Lord? or who shall stand in his holy place?"* (KJV)

As a matter of fact, several of the psalms were sung or recited as the people ascended Mount Zion to the place of worship. But nothing really happened unless they arrived at the hill of the Lord. You see, something happens in our ascension.

The Bible says that when Jesus came, He stopped. This tells me that when we are prepared, God will stop everything He is doing just to pay attention to us.

Jesus stopped at that sycamore tree. At this very moment, to those of you who have already climbed the tree, Jesus is stopping right where you are now.

The Bible says that Jesus looked up into the tree and spoke to Zacchaeus in a way that said, "I want you to come down. You have already done your part, but I want you to come down because there is something I want to do for you that only I can do: today I want to come to your house."

In other words, Jesus was saying to the tree climber, "The change you have anticipated, the change you have longed for, the change you need, that change is here. That change is about to take effect as you humbly come down."

Many of us have run ahead, gained an access point, and moved up. And we think that's it. I want to inform you that was just the first part. There is always more to God, always more to the journey God is calling us to take. There is always more in the direction the Father wants us to go. There is always some place deeper where God wants to take you. Take for example the case of Jabez. He prayed,

> *Oh that thou wouldest bless me indeed, and enlarge my coast, and that thine hand might be with me, and that thou wouldest keep me from evil, that it may not grieve me! And God granted him that which he requested.*
>
> —I Chronicles 4:10, KJV

Jabez understood that there is always more to God.

Jesus said, "Zacchaeus, come on down from that tree and let us go to your house." I want to put this into context. The change Zacchaeus needed wasn't just a change that was going to occur in his own eyes. The change had to occur in his house.

The change you need isn't just a change that will take place in your eyes, either. It will take place in your house, your home, your body, your temple. In pursuit of the change, you may go to a church or a sanctuary. You may do many wonderful things like praise and lift up your hands. You may fellowship with people, but unless you come down and open your heart and say, "Jesus, please come in and sup with me," the change is not going to come.

I have news for someone today who is reading this book right now. There is a change that Jesus wants to give you, and the change isn't going to take place in your spiritual sycamore tree. The tree, as important as it was, is just the starting point. Many of us would believe that Zacchaeus saw Jesus, and Jesus saw Zacchaeus, so that was good enough. But Jesus had a greater plan than just letting Zacchaeus be in the tree.

Jesus has a greater plan for you than just allowing you to climb a tree. Some of you have climbed many trees, spiritually speaking. But there is a level of change to receive, another level of assurance and deliverance to experience. Your feet have walked out onto the water, but you are still in a wilderness. You have left Egypt and you are now on your way to the Promised Land. There is more!

There is more than just allowing a branch to be placed in the bitter water, making it safe to drink. There is more to finding a tree planted next to the rivers of water. The Bible says that there is so much more that has to happen for that tree, meaning that the tree has to come to a stage whereby it can bring forth fruit.

Now, Zacchaeus wasn't going to bring forth fruit on that tree. As good a position as he was in, he wouldn't have been able to be fruitful there. He didn't yet have a testimony. Zacchaeus could have praised himself or patted himself on the back and said that he himself had been able to devise this great plan to run ahead and climb a tree to see Jesus. He might have felt that he had done it all himself.

I want to tell somebody that this requires more than just our exercises of worship, more than prayer or a prophetic word. God wants to do something greater in your life. He wants us to come down from our heights, from everything we have accomplished, and take Him to our home.

The Bible says that when Jesus went to Zacchaeus, He said, *"I must abide at thy house"*(Luke 19:5). This means that Jesus wants to come to your home so that He may have fellowship with you. It is a typology of the Spirit taking control. When Jesus looked at Zacchaeus as he descended from the tree in haste, He said, *"This day is salvation come to this house, forsomuch as he also is a son of Abraham"*(Luke 19:9, KJV).

In other words, salvation had come to his house, and the challenges Zacchaeus had faced were no more. He had received total deliverance, salvation, freedom, and liberty. Every negative experience that had affected Zacchaeus had become null and void. His sins, his shortcomings, and his mishaps were forgiven, because Jesus had produced a change in him. The tree couldn't have brought to him the change he needed. Not even a crowd could have brought all this to him, nor even his own energy, as good as his efforts were. The only way Zacchaeus was going to experience salvation was by Jesus coming to his house.

There is a deliverance you need to experience, and once you experience it you will be able to walk past the challenges you encountered before. You will supersede them. You will be able to stand above them. Why is that so? Because Jesus's salvation has come to your house and your heart, as it did for Zacchaeus. Jesus not only went to his house but also entered into his heart. Something took place in Zacchaeus that rendered his challenges precursors to his change; they were just stepping stones.

Today, I want you to know that all the things you are facing right now are just stepping stones on the way to your change. Something is going to change for you, and it's changing for you right now.

You have to come to the place where you say, "This challenge is going to present me its own unique form of change. I can never be the same again, because I'm having an experience that will set me up for a change."

Remember, the beginning is often challenging. People, situations, and circumstances can evolve into various shades of unpredictable, uncomfortable challenges. Yet with the right desires, one can foster a solid decision, one which enlightens the mind, emboldens the heart, empowers the feet, and simultaneously ignites blazing momentum. Learning to let the challenges of life work in our favor demands clear direction and rooted diligence.

In the final analysis, prolific and lasting change only comes after we've boldly handled and overcome all the surmountable odds. And if at last there remains any other challenge, may we all be strong enough to experience the blessings through change.

Conclusion

Remember that every challenge is unique to the individual who encounters it. Every challenge provides a point at which we can use our imagination, the leading of the voice of the Lord, and gain some sort of leverage over our trying situation. Challenges, no matter how big or small they are, have the potential to make us far better than we are now. They are character-builders in our lives once we embrace them and move through them with reasonable judgment and tact.

Your change is closer than it was yesterday. As a matter of fact, your change is here, because you have recognized that you have a way forward despite what may be limiting you and causing a level of dysfunction in your life.

Your change, and the dimensions of your change, is predicated on your ability to overcome your challenges. Make this your life's goal to rise and effectively handle everything you're faced with. Learn from your challenges, then go on to live a life of positive and lasting change.

Welcome, challenge! Welcome, change!

For more information, contact:

Potter's Vessel International
P. O. Box 120927
Brooklyn, NY 11212
office phone: 718-484-0928

Connect, sign up for email communiques,
visit the following websites:

www.trueliferadio.net · www.framptonpaul.com

Email:
frampton@trueliferadio.net · info@trueliferadio.net

CPSIA information can be obtained
at www.ICGtesting.com
Printed in the USA
LVHW032233190221
679369LV00005B/435

9 781486 616992